P9-AFZ-046

WITHDRAWN

JUL 09 2024

DAVID O. McKAY LIBRARY
BYU-IDAHO

RICKS COLLEGE
DAVID O. McKAY LIBRARY
REXBURG, IDAHO 83440

The Art of
Oboe Reed Making

Melvin Berman
University of Toronto

Illustrations by Lesley Young

Canadian Scholars' Press Inc. Toronto 1988

The Art of Oboe Reed Making

First published in 1988 by
Canadian Scholars' Press Inc.
211 Grenadier Rd.,
Toronto M6R 1R9
Canada

Original material copyright © Melvin Berman, 1988.
All Rights Reserved. No reproduction, copy or transmission of this publication may be made without written permission.

Canadian Cataloguing in Publication Data:
Main entry under title:

The Art of Oboe Reed Making

Includes index
ISBN 0-921-627-18-1

1. Oboe — Reeds.
2. Oboe — Construction. I. Title.

ML941.B47 1987   788'.72   C87-095352-4

TABLE OF CONTENTS

LIST OF DIAGRAMS

The Author

Melvin Berman, Canada's foremost oboist, is Professor of Music at the Faculty of Music of the University of Toronto. Mr. Berman has performed under the baton of the world's most distinguished conductors, including Charles Munch, Pierre Monteux, Erich Leinsdorf, Georg Solti, Zubin Mehta, John Barbirolli, Sir Thomas Beecham, Franz-Paul Decker, Colin Davis and Pierre Boulez, to name a few. He has concertized throughout France, Belgium, the USSR, Japan, the USA and Canada.

Mr. Berman was formerly Principal Oboist of the Montreal Symphony Orchestra, a post he held for more than 15 years. He was a member of the Faculty of Music at McGill University, and Professor of Oboe and Chamber Music at the Conservatoire de Musique du Québec. Prior to that, he was Principal Oboist of the Hartford Symphony Orchestra, the New Orleans Philharmonic, the Boston Pops and the Ballet Theatre of New York.

He was founding member of the Baroque Trio of Montreal, the Pro Arte Woodwind Quintet, the Toronto Winds, the Baroque Trio of Toronto and co-founder of the Mainly Mozart Festival, and has been a member of the faculties of many of the summer music schools, including the Inter-Provincial Music Camp, Banff, and the National Youth Orchestra. Melvin Berman has recorded more than 15 albums under the Vox, RCA, CBC, Orion, Berandol and Octagon labels and has made 2 award winning films, THE OBOE REED and THE OBOE. His articles have appeared in the *Double Reed Journal* and *Fugue Magazine*. He has published one brass quintet, two woodwind octets edited by himself, and a transcription for winds of the Marcello Oboe Concerto. He is mentioned in the *Encyclopedia of Music in Canada* for his contribution to music performance, pedagogy and chamber music. His former students hold posts in most of the major music institutions in Canada.

Lesley Young is one of Canada's most successful "new generation" oboists. Born in Edmonton, she graduated from the University of Toronto Faculty of Music in 1981 where she is currently the instructor of the oboe classes. Ms. Young plays oboe and english horn for the National Ballet and the Canadian Opera and is very active in all aspects of musical life in Toronto, including films, recordings and chamber music. In addition to her outstanding ability as a musician she is also an excellent illustrator, as demonstrated in *The Art of Oboe Reed Making*.

This book is dedicated to my students who have made all of my efforts worthwhile.

M.B.

I would like to thank Lesley Young for her untiring, invaluable assistance and encouragement. She not only prepared all of the diagrams but also typed the manuscript into the computer making important suggestions and improvements all along the way. This is her book as much as it is mine.

M.B.

Preface

As every oboist knows, an oboe cannot be played well without a "good" reed, and a reed cannot be considered to be good unless it does *everything* well! A reed upon which a beautiful tone can be produced but which is unresponsive in the low register is not a good reed. A reed which responds well but is impossible to play in tune is not a good reed. Only a reed which allows the player to produce a beautiful tone, excellent intonation, smooth connections, ease of response in all registers and is not excessively tiring to play may be considered a good reed. Nothing less will do. The purpose of this manual is to guide, recommend and suggest. Nothing printed in the following pages should be construed as being absolute. Flexibility and accommodation are the key words. There are simply too many "right" ways to make good reeds to be dogmatic in approaching the subject. This fact is attested to by the many thousands of wonderful oboists performing so beautifully throughout the world — each on a personal and individualized reed unique only to him or herself. If you are flexible enough to understand that there must be accommodation and adjustment to suit individual requirements, and you have the imagination and patience to experiment, you will succeed.

THE ART OF OBOE REED MAKING

I. INTRODUCTION

NOTE: *The beginner may wish to read the following sections concerning gouging and shaping in a more or less cursory manner for background purposes, returning to them at a later date for a more in-depth consideration after the decision to acquire a shaper and/or gouging machine has been made.*

Although it is possible to make reeds beginning at any stage from tube cane to a partially finished reed, the advanced player generally prefers to begin reed making with either cane in tubes, purchasable by the pound or kilo, or with already split and roughly gouged cane (approximately .8mm in thickness). For the beginning reed maker it is advisable to start making reeds with cane which has already been gouged, shaped and folded ready to be tied onto the staple (reed tube), postponing the processes of shaping and gouging cane until the basics of reed scraping have been, more or less, mastered (See Section IV., page 11, *TYING OR MOUNTING THE REED*). When ordering cane at this stage ask for the best available cane. The cane should be (1) gouged, shaped and folded; (2) of medium thickness (approximately .58 - .60 mm); and (3) of medium width (approximately 7 mm at the tip).

The diameter of the tube of cane should be between 10.5 and 11 mm. This specification is of the utmost importance, since the diameter of the cane, more than any other factor, determines the opening of the finished reed, although it is possible to affect the opening to a limited extent by scraping certain areas of the reed. This and other reed adjustments will be discussed later. For the moment, let me say that the smaller the diameter of the tube of cane, the more open the finished reed will be. The larger the diameter, the more closed will be the reed opening.

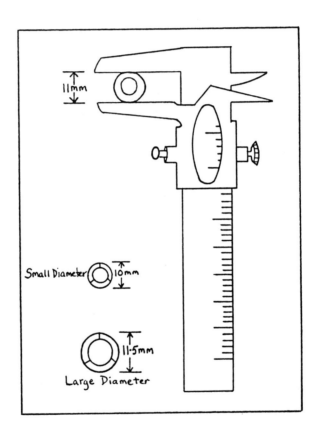

#1 Caliper measuring diameter of tube cane
Small diameter cane and arc
Large diameter cane and arc

Introduction

Since, in the final analysis, the most important single factor in making a good, vibrant, responsive, high quality oboe reed is the quality of the cane, it follows that it is extremely important to obtain the best quality cane available. It is exceedingly difficult, if not altogether impossible, to make a good reed from poor quality cane.

Where do we find good cane? This is a question that oboe players as well as bassoonists, clarinetists, and saxophone players have been asking for decades.

Most good cane comes from the southern part of France and can be purchased either through a local music store or directly from France. It can be bought at any stage of processing, from cane in round tubes as it comes from the tree to cane which has been gouged, shaped and folded ready to mount on to the reed tube (or staple) in preparation for scraping. The least expensive way to buy cane is in tubes by weight, and the cost increases as the degree of processing increases.

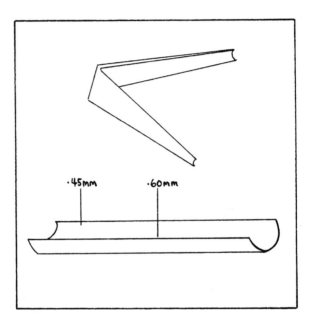

#2 Gouged cane
(.6 mm in centre .45 mm on sides)

II. GOUGING

The oboe reed making process begins with the splitting and gouging of the cane in preparation for shaping and mounting. The tube cane is split into three equal sections. This can be accomplished with the help of a splitting tool, or a reed knife. I prefer a knife so that I can eliminate, if necessary, the warped sections of cane. It is essential that the pieces of cane used to make reeds are as straight as possible, otherwise the opening of the reed may be uneven or the reed may not close properly at the sides.

4

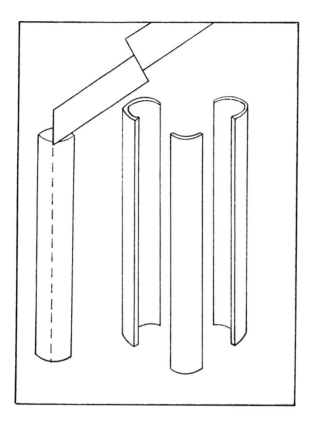

#3 Split Cane

After splitting, the cane must be soaked for 4 or 5 hours. Using the guillotine, which is usually built onto the gouging machine, the split pieces are cut to the proper length (approx. 75 mm) to fit into the bed of the gouging machine. It is often necessary to adjust the width of the split cane with a knife in order to accommodate either the guillotine or the gouging machine bed.

Before the final gouging is done, the cane which has already been split and cut to length, should be rough-gouged or pre-gouged. This is done by using either a pre-gouger or a gouging tool known as a *filiere*.

The final gouging is done with the gouging machine. In general it is a good idea to turn the cane in the bed of the gouging machine at least once in order to produce an even scrape.

A good thickness for the average player to use is .6 mm in the centre and .45 mm on the sides. These dimensions are, and should be, very flexible and adjustable. Experimentation is highly recommended. The gouge of the cane is a controversial and much discussed subject amongst oboists, as is the shape and the material from which the staples should be made. The specific material is of very little importance as long as it is air-tight. These variations make the playing of the oboe one of the most interesting and fascinating of all the woodwind instruments and perhaps the most interesting and fascinating of any of the instruments of the orchestra.

An essential element in reed making is uniformity. Our ideal should be the elimination of as many variables as possible. This is the reason for gouging cane ourselves instead of purchasing it already gouged. It is also the reason for shaping our own cane. It is true, as mentioned earlier, that the less processing which has taken place, the lower the cost of the cane. This factor is not of importance to the professional player, since the time and energy involved in preparing cane and making reeds could be put to much better use if it were possible to obtain the same or better results in any other way. Unfortunately, because of the many variations in individual needs, and because it

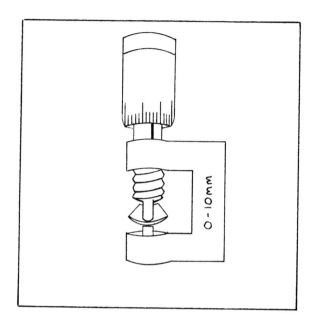

#4 Measuring cane with micrometer

appears to be commercially infeasible to meet these needs, it seems that the only sure method is the "do-it-yourself" approach.

In order to ensure one aspect of this all-important uniformity, the use of a micrometer to measure the thickness of the gouged cane is indispensible. Note that the spindle of the micrometer has been rounded in order to be able to measure the inside of the cane.

An important element in the gouging of cane is that the finished piece of cane be as smooth as possible, so that the air and moisture flow through the finished reed with a minimum of friction and restriction. It may be necessary, in some instances, to smooth the gouged cane with either very fine sandpaper or a hand gouger. In general, however, a well-sharpened gouging machine blade will do the job smoothly and efficiently without the need for additional finishing.

III. SHAPING

After the cane has been gouged, the next step in the reed making process is shaping. Be certain that the cane has been soaked in water for approximately 45 minutes.

Accurate and precise shaping can only be accomplished by the use of a perfectly symmetrical shaper, one which will hold the cane tightly in place as the shaping is being done. The first step in the shaping process is to thin the ends of the piece of gouged cane — using the easel to hold the cane. Next, score the bark with the knife following the center mark cut into the easel. Cut through the bark lightly so as not to cut into the cane itself but only through the bark. The reason for scoring the bark is to facilitate folding the cane in half, but care should be taken not to cut so deeply into the cane that the tip opens when the piece of cane is folded. It may be necessary to narrow the end of the folded piece of cane with a knife in order to allow it to fit onto the shaper. Always place the folded piece of cane carefully and evenly on the shaper and be certain that the cane is securely clamped.

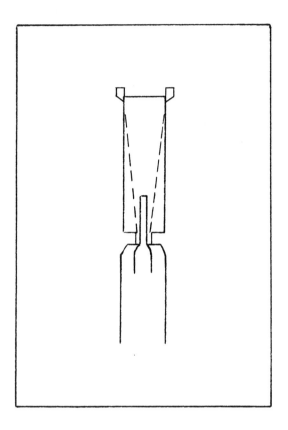

 # 5 Shaper with cane

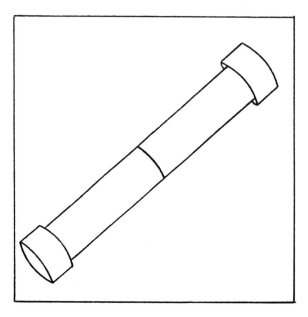

#6 Easel

WIDER SHAPER = *LOWER* PITCH AND *LARGER* REED OPENING
NARROWER SHAPER = *HIGHER* PITCH AND *SMALLER* REED OPENING

Do not use your best reed knife for shaping. A single-edged razor blade or any sharp knife will do.

MOST BEGINNER REED MAKERS START HERE

IV. TYING OR MOUNTING THE REED

We are now ready for the tying or mounting process. This is the point at which most beginning reed makers start their reed making adventure. In fact, this is the point at which most young oboists begin to make reeds, and it is usually after he or she has been making reeds for quite a while that the serious student will graduate to shaping cane. Many amateur oboists never begin before this point. This is not to minimize the importance of evenly shaped cane nor the importance of cane which is neither too narrow nor too wide, since the width of the cane in combination with uniquely individual embouchures very much influences both the pitch and the opening of the reed. Too wide a shape will tend to lower the pitch and cause certain notes to "hang" or go flat and make the extreme high register difficult to play, whereas a shape which is too narrow will raise the pitch and tend to sharpen certain notes which may be naturally inclined in that direction — such as E, F#, G, high D, and so on — depending upon the individual oboe and oboist. As a rule, I would recommend a shaper which will produce a finished reed of just under 7 mm at the tip. Again, let me say that discussion and controversy concerning shapers have been a continuing source of interesting dialogue amongst oboists since the beginning of reed making. The pros and cons of a wide shape versus a narrow shape, or what exact effects each type of shape produces, is a never-ending source of delightful conversation whenever oboe players get together.

But now onward to tying the folded and shaped cane to the staple. Remember, the cane must be soaked for approximately 45 minutes before mounting. With a piece of fine sandpaper, smooth the edges of the cane slightly to ensure a tight fit. With bees-wax, obtainable at either a drug, hardware or sewing store, wax about 24 inches of nylon thread (ff diameter) and rewind it onto a spindle — a six-inch piece of half-inch dowling will do fine. Tie one end of the nylon to a hook or small "C" clamp mounted firmly and conveniently waist-high when seated. Place the staple on the mandrel and the cane in position on the staple, with approximately 25 mm of cane extending over the top of the staple.

MORE CANE ON STAPLE = SMALLER REED OPENING

LESS CANE ON STAPLE = LARGER REED OPENING

Next, tie 2 or 3 turns of thread around the cane at about 5 or 6 turns below the top of the tube. Pull slowly and not too tightly so that you can align the cane evenly. (If the cane splits during this procedure the results may not always be detrimental, especially if the splitting is below the top of the staple. However, if the splitting runs up the reed above the nylon it may, and I emphasize *may,* cause the reed to become flat in the high register).

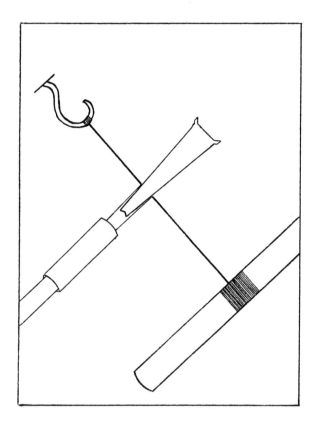

#7 Spindle, hook, reed on mandrel and nylon thread

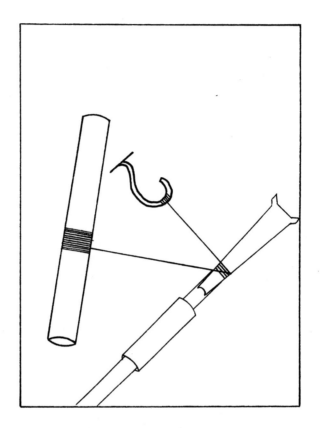

#8 Tying and the Cross-over

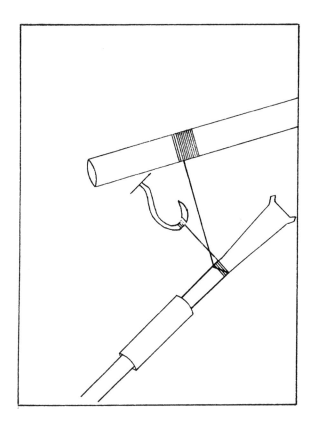

#8a The Cross-over continued

It is extremely important that the cane be vertically straight and not twisted. This can be easily accomplished using the mandrel handle as a guide. Once the cane is aligned, start wrapping the nylon around the reed tying up to, but not over, the top of the staple. Pull slowly and tightly until the cane closes evenly on the sides. Never tie over the top of the staple, and if the cane does not close at the sides, loosen the nylon and slide one more millimeter of the cane onto the staple. Always keep the thread very taut while binding and make certain that the cane remains straight and perfectly aligned.

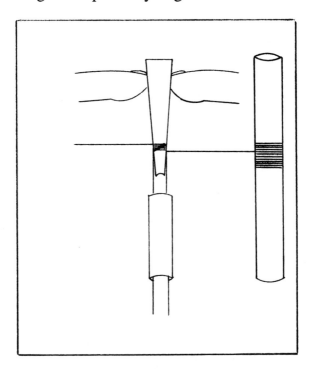

#9 Aligning the reed

Tying or Mounting the Reed

When the nylon has reached the top of the staple which is visible through the light, reverse direction by crossing over the nylon strand fastened to the hook or clamp, and wind your way down the staple to the cork, keeping the thread taut at all times. It may be necessary to loosen your grip on the cane slightly in order to re-align the cane with your forefingers, so that the reed is straight and closing evenly on both sides. When the cane is re-aligned continue as before until the nylon is down to the cork. It may feel a bit awkward at first, but after a few weeks your dexterity will improve rapidly, and in a short time you will be able to mount a reed in about two minutes or less.

Finishing the tying securely is absolutely essential, since it is quite discouraging, if not absolutely terrifying, to discover your best reed unravelling before your eyes just as you are about to start playing an important solo! The method of finishing the tying is quite simple and involves the use of 3 or 4 half-hitches as close to the cork as possible, making certain that the binding does not unravel before the first half-hitch is secured. Some players put a drop of cement or clear fingernail polish on the half-hitches to prevent them from loosening, but I have never found this necessary especially if the nylon is well waxed before tying. Once the cane is bound and finished securely, cut off the "ears" and even the sides with a file.

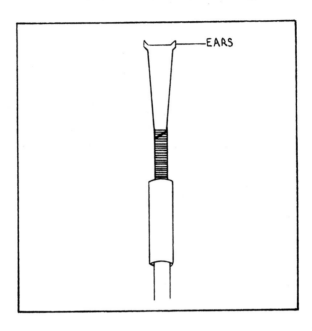

#10 Ears

At this point I must once again emphasize the importance of evenness and symmetry. An uneven, unsymmetrical, crooked reed will, generally speaking, not respond evenly, and will not perform as well as an even, symmetrical reed. Some players prepare several "blanks" at one sitting and stock-pile them for future scraping. My preference is to proceed with the scraping process immediately.

V. SCRAPING - STAGE 1

We are now ready to proceed to the first stage of the scraping process. Use a mandrel every step of the way from the mounting and binding to the very last scrape. This will ensure better control of the knife and more stable support of the reed as you

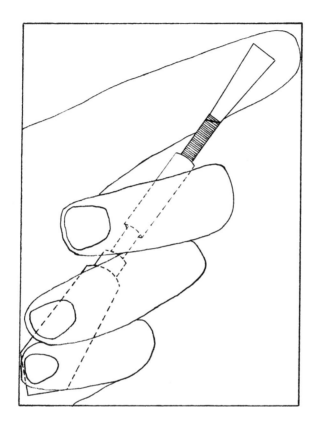

#11 Holding the reed utilizing mandrel

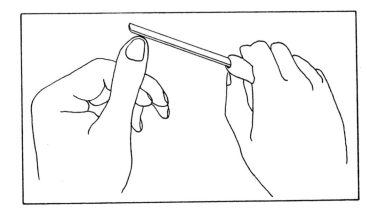

#12 Thumb as a fulcrum

work on it. Please take note of the manner in which the knife is held and used — especially of the wrist action and the use of the thumb as a fulcrum.

Enough downward pressure must be exerted in order to scrape a reasonable amount of cane at each stroke. Always scrape away from you. With a little experimentation and practice you will soon accommodate yourself to the downward pressure and hand technique required. An important factor to remember is to keep the knife sharp at all times. It will be necessary to sharpen your knife occasionally while making reeds. This will be determined by whether or not enough cane is being removed without requiring undue pressure or pulling. If in doubt about whether or not the knife needs sharpening,

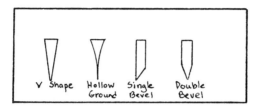

#13 Knives

sharpen it! I must emphasize that it is essential to have more than one knife. Very often one knife will not scrape a particular reed very well, while another knife will perform beautifully. Furthermore, for cutting off the tip on the block, only a "V"-shaped knife or single-edged razor blade can be used successfully.

Begin by scraping the reed approximately 10 mm on the side of the tip and 5 mm in the centre in order to initiate as early as possible the inverted "U"-shaped pattern, keeping in mind that the tip will loose about 1 or 2 mm when it is cut off on the block. Inspect the reed very often through a strong backlight making certain that both sides of the reed are always equally scraped. This equality or balance must be carried out throughout the reed making procedure. Always keep in mind the key word — symmetry.

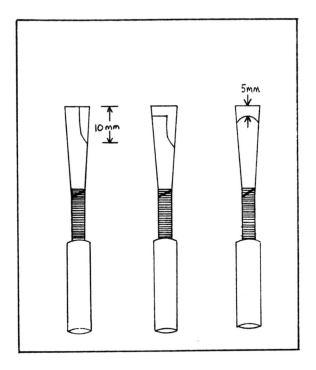

#14 Beginning scrapes

Next, we scrape the four sides. Yes, four sides! (A reed in the style that we are making and which is in general use by most North American oboists actually has ten basic areas. They include the tip, the two sides, the heart, and the spine. And since we are dealing with a double reed, double the areas, and we have ten). We scrape the four sides evenly, inspecting our progress through the light, making long, smooth scrapes. Keep in mind at this point that we are simply scraping the sides and studiously avoiding the spine. Be careful not to scrape all the way to the very edge of the sides but rather leave a thin edge of bark running down almost to the tip. These so-called "rails" can be adjusted or almost eliminated in future, final adjustments. But for the moment they should remain.

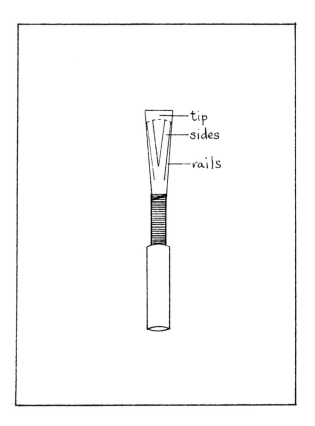

#14a Sides and Rails

Although the separate areas of the reed (tip, spine, heart, sides, back) must be very well defined and readily visible through the light, it is best to terrace or blend the sections smoothly into one another rather than having each individual section end abruptly and another begin. Terracing tends to unify, darken, and enrich the tone colour much like a beautiful fall landscape, whereas, abrupt and angular scraping produces a more edgy, harsh, and wooden quality.

At this point we have progressed to a reed with sides almost completely finished and a tip which has yet to be opened. We should now, lightly and carefully, remove the bark from the centre of the reed on both sides. Using the block, cut the tip so that the cane portion of the reed is approximately 23 to 24 mm in length. Attempt to produce a "crowing" sound (for which oboists throughout the world are notorious), and finally, try it in the oboe.

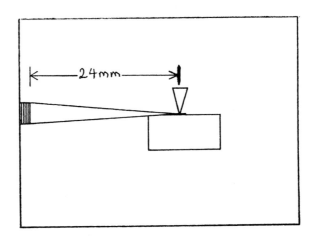

#15 Cutting tip

The "crow" will often provide a good indication of how the reed will finally evolve and where to scrape in order to improve the reed. For example, if the "crow" is very high pitched it is usually an indication that more cane must be removed from the back or sides of the reed, and conversely, if the "crow" is low, hollow and raucous, it is generally an indication that too much wood has been removed from the centre and back. Experimentation at this juncture is essential, since an oboe reed

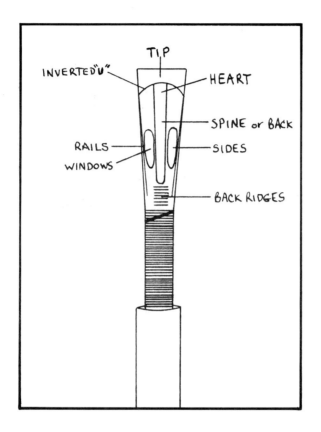

#16 Finished reed

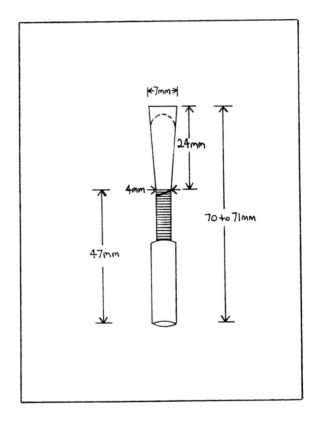

#16a Dimensions

is so uniquely personal. A little later I will illustrate the major reed problems and possible solutions.

After testing the semi-finished reed in the oboe you will have found that the sound produced was probably somewhat stuffy (muffled), dull and/or hard, lacking in warmth, centre or

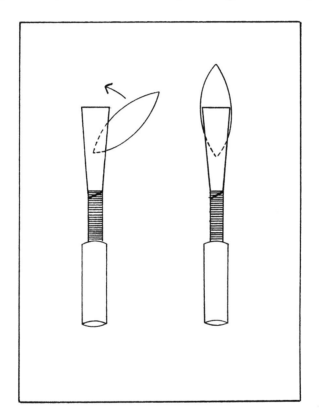

#17 Inserting plaque from side

ring (vibrancy). Now, insert the plaque and scrape the tip, sides and centre minimally and carefully. I must emphasize that very little cane should be removed at this time. We are simply finishing the first stage of the scrape, and the basic rule of reed making should always remain uppermost in mind, i.e., *cane can always be removed but never replaced.*

At this point the reed should be set aside and allowed to dry overnight before proceeding to the second stage. It is best not to finish a reed in one sitting. Always give the cane an opportunity to dry out, recuperate and assume its new shape after each stage. The entire reed making process should take 3 or 4 days or even longer for best results. Finishing reeds where you will be using them such as the stage, pit or rehearsal room is always a good idea.

VI. SCRAPING — STAGE 2

Assuming that the reed has been left to dry overnight, we are now ready to proceed to the second stage. Firstly, wet the reed by dipping it into *hot water* of at least 100 degrees fahrenheit and then replace it in the reed box. After 10 minutes the reed will be ready to work with — either to play or to continue scraping. Eliminate excess water and blow into the reed producing a sound or "crow" in order to vibrate the cane. Insert the plaque and mandrel and start thinning the tip — emphasizing and delineating, even more pronouncedly, the inverted "U"shape. Continue to work in this area until the tip is quite thin and clear and the "U" shape is very distinctly defined. Next, thin the four sides, always removing the same amount of cane on each side, or where necessary, more or less from one side or another in order to maintain the same thickness on each side. Now, scrape a small amount from the centre or spine using a long, smooth scrape and retaining an over-all taper from tube to tip. Always bear in mind that the reed is divided into five basic areas (ten when doubled) each of which has its very own function and thickness: the tip which is the thinnest, followed by the sides which should be next in thickness, and finally the heart and spine which are the thickest.

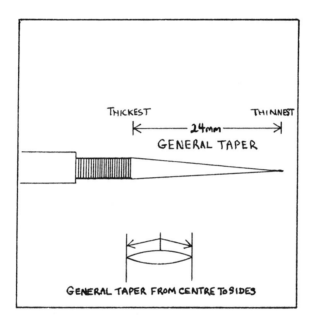

#18 General taper

As you work, inspect the reed often through the light and occasionally blow through the reed to make it "crow" or simply to produce a sound.

It would now be a good idea to try the reed in the oboe. This is always an exciting moment.

Two reminders are appropriate at this time. (1) Always keep your knife sharp, and (2) maintain a general taper from back to tip and from centre to sides.

An additional point concerning the "crow" is that if you can produce a "crow" which sounds an approximate "C" in octaves it is a good indication that you are going in the right direction. However, I must say that I have made very good reeds with poor "crows" and vice versa.

At this time put the reed aside once again, and allow it to dry and recuperate overnight.

VII. SCRAPING — STAGE 3 (FINAL STAGE)

The final stage in the scraping process is really an adjustment period and therefore requires a light and delicate scraping technique — more or less allowing the weight of the knife along with only a slight downward hand pressure — to accomplish the desired results. Although it may seem redundant and simplistic to repeat the rule, "cane can always be removed but never replaced," it is, nevertheless, worth mentioning again, since the abrogation of this rule and poor quality cane are the two most frequent causes of reed making failures. This stage involves "playing in" or "breaking in" the reed and making any final adjustments which might be required in order to improve response, intonation and tone quality. (A tuning fork or any tuning device which will sound an "A"- 440 must be in the tool collection of every oboist.) This adjustment period should be spaced over a day or two. Since the reed changes as it is being played, it is advisable to play a reed, make a few adjustments, and then set the reed aside until the following day — following this procedure for perhaps two or three days. It is wise to have three or four reeds in progress at all times and at different stages. Never allow yourself to be left with only one good reed!

VIII. PROBLEMS AND SOLUTIONS

Although the inherent properties of the cane, combined with the gouge and the shape, ultimately determine the final quality of the reed, much can be done to rectify many reed problems. Some of the most common of these problems can often be corrected or improved by scraping or trimming the proper areas of the reed.

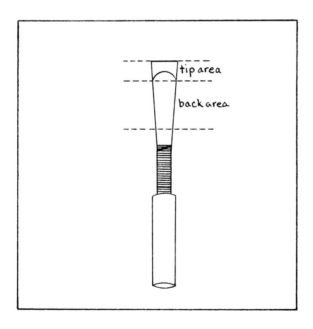

#19 Tip and back areas

GENERAL PRINCIPLE:

Scraping the *tip* area *brightens* the tone and helps the *high* register
Scraping the *back* area *darkens* the tone and helps the *low* register

1) NON-RESPONSIVE LOW REGISTER

If the low register does not respond well, scrape the back and sides as well as a small amount from just behind the tip (heart). This will also tend to darken the sound and perhaps produce a warmer, richer tone quality. If, however, too much cane is removed from the back and sides, the reed may collapse resulting in a flat upper register. "G" and "F"# may hang, meaning that it will be extremely difficult to bring these notes up to pitch without excessive pinching or tightening of the embouchure, and the very high register will be difficult to play.

One further point concerning a non-responsive low register. If the reed does not open enough, the low notes may be difficult to produce. The major determining factor governing reed opening is the diameter of the tube of cane from which the particular piece of cane was taken. For example, if the diameter is very large — let us say 12 mm — then the finished reed will have a small opening, since the arc from large diameter cane will be considerably smaller, and of course reeds made from cane of a small diameter such as 10 mm, will tend to be too open. The best average diameter in a temperate climate at medium sea-level is 11 mm (See Diagram # 1).

2) REED OPENING

Suppose we have a finished reed which is relatively good in most respects, except that the opening is too closed. Is the situation hopeless? No. Although it is much better to have a reed with an opening which is correct because the dimensions of the cane are right, it *is* possible to adjust the opening to a certain extent by adjusting the staple of the finished reed with pliers. Flattening or compressing the staple at the points indicated in Diagram #20 will close the reed and in Diagram #21 will open the reed. It should be noted that this procedure will probably destroy the staple for future use and so should be reserved for emergencies only.

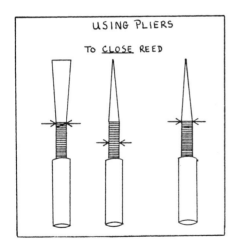
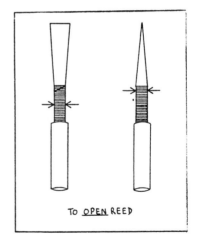

#20 Using pliers to close the reed
#21 Using pliers to open the reed

3) SLIDING THE BLADES

The technique of sliding the bottom blade of the reed slightly to the right is sometimes, often, never or always used (depending upon your advisor) to reduce the opening of the reed and stabilize the pitch. I find this technique useful only if the reed is too open and/or the pitch has a tendency to hang. The effect is, in fact, the same that would be achieved by the use of a narrower shape and larger diameter cane. This, of course, is not possible once the reed is made, whereas sliding the blades is.

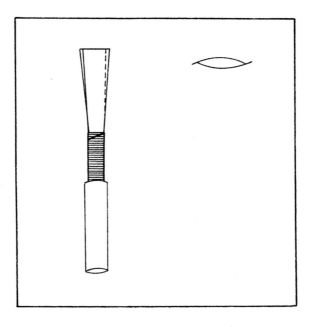

#22 Sliding the blades

Another important factor worth mentioning concerning the reed opening is its effect on dynamic range. A reed with a very small opening will allow for only the slightest amount of pressure both of air and of embouchure before closing, especially if the quality of the cane is soft and lacking in springiness.

Therefore, a very small opening will inhibit forte playing, although I must say that a small opening is to be preferred over one which is too large to control and which requires excessive embouchure pressure (biting). A final consideration relative to the reed opening is its effect on pitch. A small opening tends to raise the general pitch, while a large opening often lowers it, especially in the high register. And finally — a reed which is too open for one player may be too closed for another.

4) HIGH REGISTER PROBLEMS

If the high notes, meaning high "C" and up, are difficult to produce, the problem may be in the quality of the cane — too soft or soggy. However, if it is not the cane, or you are not certain, or even if it is the cane, measures can be taken. Thinning the tip often helps (See Diagram #16). Shortening the tip by cutting it the smallest fraction of a millimeter almost always improves the response of the extreme high notes. A narrow shape improves high note production and tends to raise the general pitch as does sliding the blades.

5) GENERAL PITCH TOO LOW

If the general pitch is too low, shortening the overall length of the reed will bring up the pitch. This can be done either by cutting the tip or by shortening the staple with a file. Cutting the tip often necessitates re-scraping the reed, since the entire positioning of the scrape is altered, and the balance among the various areas of the reed is changed. If raising the general overall pitch is required very often, it may be an indication that a shorter staple is needed — perhaps a 46 mm staple rather than the standard 47 mm or perhaps 23 mm of cane instead of 24 mm. A word of caution concerning the use of a shortened staple: most oboes are built to play in tune with the standard 47 mm staple. It is possible to utilize either a slightly shorter or longer staple — perhaps 1 mm more or less. However, it should be remembered that using an extremely short or long staple may also alter the relative intonation of an instrument as well as factors influencing quality of sound and responsiveness. Once the embouchure is well established experimentation is valuable, since every player has different physical characteristics, and among embouchures there is infinite diversity — even among students of the same teacher.

6) GENERAL PITCH TOO HIGH

Lowering the pitch can often be accomplished to a limited degree by scraping from the back, or from the sides toward the back, sometimes called the "windows" (See Diagrams # 16 & 26). Care should be taken not to scrape too much from this area, since, as previously mentioned, an excessive amount removed from the back may collapse the reed resulting in a hanging or flat upper register as well as a hollow, raucous tone. The use of a longer staple (48 mm or even 49 mm) is a possible solution to the problem of a chronically high-pitched instrument or reed. Another possibilty, though somewhat unorthodox, is the use of a spacer of approximately 1 mm in thickness placed in the well. One can be made by cutting off, with a small triangular file, the bottom of an old staple, being careful not to destroy the cork. Again, I must caution that if a *chronic* problem of pitch exists in either direction — high or low — often more than simply the reed is to blame. Investigate the possibility that your oboe may be an inherently low or high-pitched instrument. In which case changing the well may help somewhat. Furthermore, continued extreme sharp or flat playing is often an indication of improper embouchure formation or inadequate air support or other difficulties not directly attributable to the reed.

In general, to improve the high register adjust the tip area, and to improve the low register scrape from the back and sides. This, of couse, is an over-simplification of the entire complex procedure of reed adjustment, but it does serve as a point of departure. From this point it is only necessary to experiment in order to find your way.

7) STUFFINESS

Occasionally we find ourselves with a reed which performs rather well but is a bit stuffy, muffled or covered — not allowing enough ringing quality or vibrancy to enter the sound picture.

Overall scraping is called for here, especially thinning the tip, spine and heart in that order, and testing the reed in the oboe after each careful and thoughtful scraping.

8) REEDINESS

Reediness refers to a quality of tone which, to our ears, is excessively bright, "tippy," grainy, spread, nasal, piercing, strident, raspy or buzzy!— All nasty words to the oboist. This condition can sometimes be improved by shortening the tip and scraping the back and side areas (the "windows"). A tip which is too long and thin often exacerbates this problem. Relative to this I must make mention of what are called the rails of the reed. These, so-called rails, must be kept no matter how narrow or thin they may become in the course of finishing the reed. They serve to support the reed both physically and tonally, and though it may be necessary to nearly eliminate them in order to produce a less wooden, warmer tone quality, they should be left as an area for "last chance" adjustment of both tone and reed opening. One final cautionary comment concerning cane: each piece of cane dictates its own final scrape or structure and therefore requires, and indeed demands, its very own treatment.

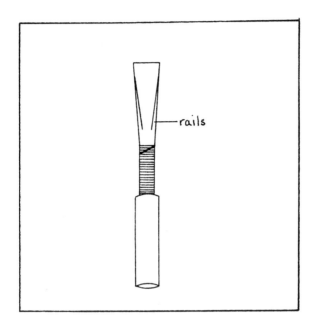

#23 The rails

IX. REED DIMENSIONS

Always strive for a reed of approximately 70 to 71 mm in total length. However, don't be overly rigid in your determination to keep to this 70 mm length. Let your oboe, ear, embouchure and tuning fork be your guide. It is, above all, absolutely essential to play in tune! Impeccable intonation must always be your goal. A prerequisite to the achievement of this goal is a fixed point of departure. This point of departure is "A"-440 cycles per second. Therefore, it is an absolute requirement to hover at all times directly over this fixed point. Most instruments made for

North American use are constructed utilizing the "A"-440 pitch centre and any deviation, other than the most minute one (1 or 2 vibrations) may result in intonation problems.

X. GOLDBEATER'S SKIN

One item which every oboist should keep in his or her oboe case is Goldbeater's skin, better known as fishskin. This thin, membrane type material is used to stop air from escaping between the two blades of the reed close to the staple. If air escapes, the reed will not respond properly especially in the low register. This can be rectified by the utilization of a small piece of fishskin (approx. 1/2 x 1 1/4 inches) moistened with your tongue and wrapped around the reed at the binding. *Naturally, the ideal is to make a reed that does not leak.*

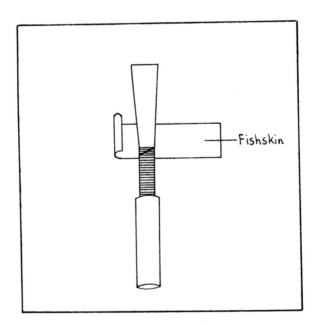

#24 Applying Fishskin

This can be done by using cane which is not warped, is properly shaped, and is bound evenly and correctly on good quality staples. Unfortuately, this ideal is not always achieved, and an occasional reed will leak.

FINAL COMMENTS

There are several other factors which must be considered in any comprehensive discussion of reeds. They are the following:

XI. HUMIDITY AND ALTITUDE

The effect of humidity on oboe reeds is enormous both in terms of sound production as well as reed opening. The higher the humidity, the more a reed will tend to open and the lower the humidity the more the reed will close, to the extent that in a greatly dehumidified or dry environment a reed may close down so much that it becomes impossible to play, and in an environment of high humidity it may open excessively, making it uncomfortable to control. It is humidity or lack of it, which affects the reed most of all.

Altitude is also an extremely influential factor in reed performance. At high altitudes a reed tends to close more than at lower altitudes. This necessitates the use of cane of smaller diameter. Low altitude and high humidity require the utilization of larger diameter cane (See Diagram # 1).

XII. PHYSICAL CHARACTERISTICS

Variations of embouchures caused by personal physical characteristics such as teeth, jaws, lips, etc. will determine the reed which each oboist will finally settle upon. This is the reason that it is so necessary for the serious oboist to have the ability and skill to make and adjust his or her own reeds.

XIII. FINISHING TOUCHES

The Sound Barrier. If a reed is playable but somewhat stuffy, muffled, and perhaps a bit unresponsive, scrape very lightly from a narrow swath of approximately 3 mm in width just behind the tip area following the contour of the inverted "U". This will allow the reed to vibrate more freely and produce a brighter and freer tone. I call this swath the Sound Barrier because before scraping in this area it often serves to bar or restrict the sound, but with a little judicious knife work the "Barrier" can be "Broken," so to speak, allowing the vibrations to flow through.

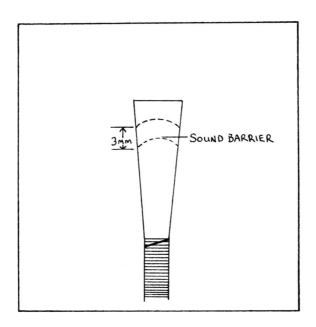

#25 The Sound Barrier

The Side Windows. The side windows are located at the back of the reed towards the sides between the rails and the spine. "Opening" these windows by scraping out a shallow valley will tend to darken and enrich the quality of sound and aid response especially in the low register. Take care to evaluate the reed thoughtfully before proceeding too hastily and enthusiastically with the windows, since opening the windows excessively may result in a collapse of the reed. This will be evidenced by a hanging and sagging of pitch overall, but especially in the high register, as well as a tone without centre or core. This can be especially devastating if the reed had been rather good before you decided to open the windows "just a little more."

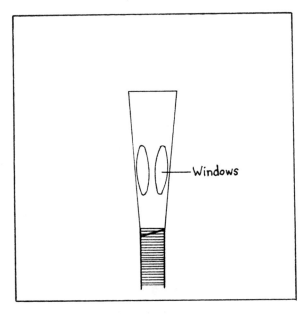

#26 The windows

The Back Ridges. As a final touch, some players utilize the back ridges to darken the tone and assist low register response. They are simply 7 or 8 very short and abrupt scrapes about 1 mm apart at the very back of the reed immediately above the nylon. They tend to remove any remaining vestiges of harshness. (I put them on all my reeds.)

#27 Back ridges

The Short "V" and the Long "V". Often a reed, which is quite good in most respects, may suggest by its general behavior in respect to either tone or response that "something more" should be done, yet it is not clear what that "something" is. What is usually needed in this case is a unifying action. Unifying in respect to connecting all the disparate areas of the reed to one another. After all, if there is a lack of sympathetic communication among the various segments of the reed, the result is literally chaos, which often manifests itself in poor response, edgy tone or merely as "something" missing.

The Short "V" and/or the Long "V" scrape is often the "final touch" which will bring all the diverse areas of the reed into communication with each other, resulting in a smoother immediate response and a richer yet more vibrant sound. This is not always a necessary step with all reeds, since in reed making the communication system is often blended into the scraping process unconciously and quite naturally. However, if it is felt that something additional would be beneficial, try the *Short "V"* first. Starting about 10 mm from the tip of the reed at a point exactly in the center of the reed, scrape very lightly 2 or 3 times to each corner. This will tend to brighten the sound and help overall response.

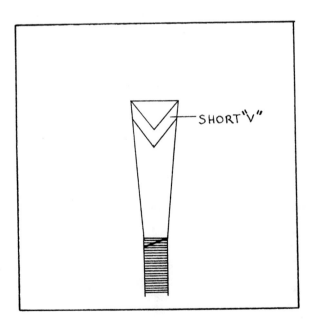

#28 The short "V"

Finishing Touches

If you wish to enrich and darken the sound somewhat and at the same time help the low register try the *Long "V"*. This involves scraping in a long, continuous light scrape a "V", starting at about 5 or 6 mm from the nylon, again in the center of the reed, and proceeding to each corner. This scrape serves to tie the entire length of the reed together encouraging it to react as one. The emphasis here is on light scraping and judicious application.

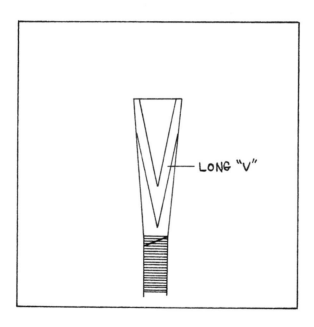

#29 The long "V"

XIV. THE ENGLISH HORN REED

The wire.   The english horn reed is nothing more than an enlargement of the oboe reed with some slight modifications including the use of the wire (24-gauge soft brass) to control the opening of the reed and give it more stability. It is best applied to the reed after most of the basic scraping has been done, and the reed has been opened and left to dry out overnight. In this way it does not interfere with the scraping process, nor does it inhibit the reed from seeking its natural formation. It is, however, possible to put it on immediately after tying on the cane or at any other time and still achieve good results. The wire should always be used on english horn reeds, since it noticeably stabilizes the reed and offers control of the opening. Because of the size of the english horn reed, it is not detrimental to the tone as it might be if applied to the oboe reed.

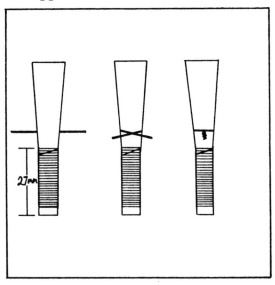

#30 Applying english horn wire

To fasten the wire to the reed cut a short length of wire (approx. 30 mm) and place it under the reed at not more than 4 mm above the nylon thread so as not to throttle the reed and choke the sound. Bring the two ends of the wire together close to the reed and twist them once. Then, with your needle-nose pliers continue to twist the wire several more times until it is wound snugly against the reed but is not squeezing into it. Cut the resulting excess twisted wire to about 3 mm and turn the end down toward the nylon, flattening it against the reed. Smooth out any sharp points or edges of the wire with a file to avoid cutting your lip. If the wire has loosened after the reed has dried out, there is no cause for alarm. Simply push it back up the reed so that it again fits snugly and firmly.

The mandrel and staple. Always use an english horn mandrel rather than an oboe mandrel when making english horn reeds and utilize staples which fit snugly on the bocal at about 10 mm, making certain that there is no air leakage between the staple and the bocal. To ensure that there is no leakage use a short length of aquarium tubing (approx. 10 mm) as a connecting sleeve between the reed and the bocal. Slip about 5 mm of tubing over the end of the staple and when putting the reed onto the bocal, simply insert the bocal into the other end of the tubing and press the reed firmly onto the bocal as far as it will go.

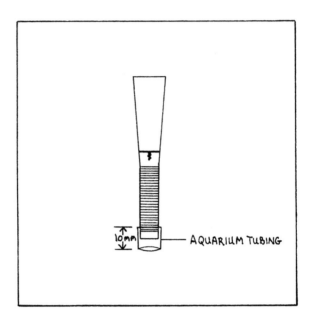

#31 Aquarium tubing

Tying. The method of tying an english horn reed is no different from that of tying an oboe reed. However, always finish tying an english horn reed 3 or 4 mm above the end of the staple so as to allow space for the tubing to slide on. When tying on the cane consider that the *finished reed* should be approximately 55 mm to 57 mm in *overall* length. The width of the shaped cane should be about 8.25 mm. Too wide a shape may cause difficulties with high notes and exacerbate other problems unique to the english horn. A good gouge thickness is .75 mm in the centre and .6 mm on the sides. (The side measurement of .6 mm is only relevant if you are gouging your own cane.) The length of english horn cane before folding should be approximately 92 mm.

Scraping.   Scraping the english horn reed is essentially the same as for the oboe reed. However, more cane may be removed immediately behind the tip in order to allow for more vibrancy and freedom, and since the english horn is inherently a much darker sounding instrument, more cane may be removed in general with good tonal and responsive results.

From the point of view of embouchure the english horn is somewhat less tiring to play relative to the oboe, which is attributable to the fact that the reed is larger and therefore less taxing to control.

XV. KNIFE SHARPENING

Good reeds cannot be made with a dull reed knife. Sharpening a knife is a very simple process and takes only a minute or less. Using a very fine stone (about the abrasiveness of this page) pour a small amount of light oil of the viscosity of 3 in 1 oil on to the surface of the stone. With your knife, spread the oil so that it covers the area which will be utilized in the sharpening procedure. Place the knife flat on the stone gently and begin to rotate it in a circular motion counter-clockwise. After about 8 or 9 circles using only moderate pressure continue the rotations while slightly lifting the back of the blade until a change of sound is detected. This change of sound indicates that the sharpening is occurring. Do not lift the back too high (not more than 1 or 2 mm) since this may result in dulling the edge rather that sharpening it, and do not sharpen too long — not more than 15 or 20 circular movements. Press a bit more as you move away from the edge of the blade and lighten up as you round the circle and head back towards the edge. Now turn the knife over and

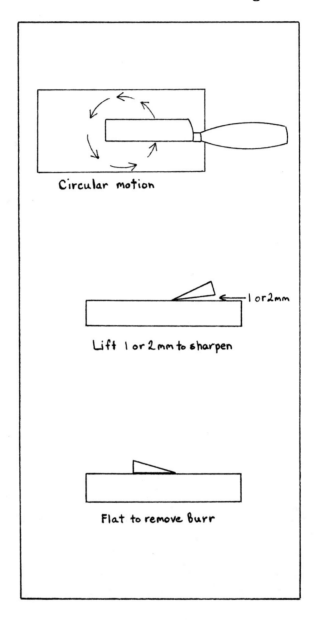

Circular motion

Lift 1 or 2mm to sharpen

Flat to remove Burr

#32 Sharpening knife

gently remove the burr which will have been produced on the opposite side of the blade. This burr must be removed to complete the sharpening of the knife and is easily accomplished by a few gentle strokes of the blade flat against the stone either straight or in a circular motion as before. Always wipe the blade clean before continuing to scrape the reed. If the knife does not perform to your satisfaction after sharpening, use a different knife for the time being or repeat the sharpening process.

CONCEPT

Finally, it remains to be said that each player's personal concept of the tone quality which he or she is striving to produce will inevitably be the overriding force which will determine the reed scrape and style.

With reed making as in any other endeavor, to rise above the mediocre, it is necessary to take risks. Don't be afraid to experiment and take chances with your reeds. Many oboists play reeds which are unfinished simply because they do not know when a reed is finished and are fearful to experiment. It is not possible to know when a reed is finished until you have gone "too far" in every area of the scrape many times. Only in this way can you determine what is excessive for your unique embouchure and requirements.

The factors which determine the kind and style of reed each individual oboist will finally arrive at are precisely those factors which make each human being just a bit different from another. Questions of taste, opinion, personal tonal concept, environment, language spoken, early musical influences, physical characteristics — all these extremely personal peculiarities — will, in the final analysis, determine the end result. Every oboist finally arrives at his or her own unique reed.

There is no magic involved in successful reed making. What is required are good tools, good light, the best cane available, an optimistic approach and much patience.

INDEX

55

Index

Index

Index

3851